CULTURE
in the Kitchen

FOODS OF
the Middle East

By Roman Ayter

Gareth Stevens
Publishing

Please visit our website, www.garethstevens.com. For a free color catalog of all our high-quality books, call toll free 1-800-542-2595 or fax 1-877-542-2596.

Library of Congress Cataloging-in-Publication Data

Ayter, Roman.
Foods of the Middle East / Roman Ayter.
    p. cm. — (Culture in the kitchen)
Includes bibliographical references and index.
ISBN 978-1-4339-5720-8 (pbk.)
ISBN 978-1-4339-5721-5 (6-pack)
ISBN 978-1-4339-5718-5 (library binding)
  1. Diet—Middle East—Juvenile literature. 2. Cooking, Middle Eastern—Juvenile literature. 3. Food—Middle East—Juvenile literature. 4. Food habits—Middle East—Juvenile literature. I. Title.
TX360.M628A98 2011
641.5956—dc22

                                        2010052688

First Edition

Published in 2012 by
Gareth Stevens Publishing
111 East 14th Street, Suite 349
New York, NY 10003

Copyright © 2012 Gareth Stevens Publishing

Designer: Daniel Hosek
Editor: Therese Shea

Photo credits: Cover and all interior images Shutterstock.com.

Printed in the United States of America

CPSIA compliance information: Batch #CS11GS: For further information contact Gareth Stevens, New York, New York at 1-800-542-2595.

Contents

Words in the glossary appear in **bold** type the first time they are used in the text.

Where Asia Meets Africa

The Middle East is the area where southwestern Asia meets northeastern Africa. Its many countries include Bahrain, Egypt, Iran, Iraq, Israel, Jordan, Kuwait, Lebanon, Oman, Qatar, Saudi Arabia, Syria, Turkey, the United Arab Emirates, and Yemen.

About 370 million people live in the Middle East. More than three-fourths are Arabs who speak the Arabic language. However, Iranians speak Persian, which is sometimes called Farsi. Turkish is spoken in Turkey, and Israelis speak Hebrew. There are many more **cultures** and languages in the Middle East.

Turkey

Lebanon   Syria

Israel

Jordan   Iraq   Iran

Kuwait

Egypt   Saudi Arabia   Bahrain
Qatar

United Arab
Emirates   Oman

Yemen

Other countries sometimes labeled as
Middle Eastern are Afghanistan, Algeria, Cyprus,
Libya, Morocco, Pakistan, Sudan, and Tunisia.

Food with a History

The Middle East is called the birthplace of **civilization**. More than 10,000 years ago, people began to farm there. The first system of writing was created there, too.

Early Arab tribes drank goat's milk and ate foods such as dates and nuts. Persians ate fruits, rice, and meat such as duck. As tribes **bartered** with people outside the Middle East, they adopted foods from other places as their own. For example, yogurt from Russia and spices from India and China became important parts of many Middle Eastern dishes.

Another Bite

Middle Eastern farmers feared locusts, which are insects that eat crops. However, they also cooked and ate the locusts!

Sometimes Middle Eastern cooks mix spices for a special taste. Za'atar is a mix of spices used on meats, vegetables, rice, and breads.

Farming and Crops

Throughout its history, much of the land of the Middle East was hot and dry. This made it hard to grow food. Some of the best farmland was near rivers, such as the Tigris and the Euphrates Rivers in Iraq and the Nile River in Egypt. Today, dams, **irrigation**, and farm machinery make it easier to grow crops in many more places.

The main crops of the Middle East are wheat, corn, rice, and **barley**. People also grow olives, dates, grapes, tomatoes, and apples. Eggplant is the most popular vegetable.

Another Bite

The country of Yemen grows coffee and sells much of it overseas. A popular coffee drink is named for its port city, Mocha.

In this photo of farmland along the Euphrates River, it's easy to see the difference between irrigated and dry soil.

Common Foods

Middle Eastern food is known for its **fragrant** spices. Other common **ingredients** include honey, sesame seeds, and chickpeas. Rice probably first arrived from India. Now it's eaten every day in countries such as Iran, Saudi Arabia, and Iraq.

challah

While many meals are served without meat in the Middle East, bread is always on the table. Pita is a flat bread that can be opened and filled with food. Other breads include the Jewish braided bread challah and an Arabic barley bread called fatir.

Another Bite

Saffron is a yellow Middle Eastern spice that comes from flowers. It's the most expensive spice in the world, costing more than $600 a pound (.5 kg)!

In the dish called hummus, chickpeas (also called garbanzo beans) are mashed or blended until the mixture is smooth. Pita bread is pictured at the top of the page.

Meze

In some Middle Eastern countries such as Turkey and Jordan, restaurants offer a good way to taste many foods in a single meal. Meze is a group of small dishes. Olives and pickles are often part of the selection. Baba ganoush is a creamy dip made of eggplant and sesame seeds. Hummus is another popular meze dish. Dolmas are grape leaves stuffed with meat and rice. Nuts may also be served, as well as vegetables. Several meze dishes are becoming popular in the United States.

Middle Eastern foods may be called different names. In some Arabic countries, the meze meal is called muqabbilat.

Meats

The kinds of meats eaten in the Middle East often depend on **religion**. People who practice the Jewish and Muslim religions don't eat pork. Lamb, however, is popular. People who live near the Persian Gulf—such as those in Bahrain and Kuwait—enjoy fish.

Like other Middle Eastern foods, meat is often spiced. Spiced meat is called kofta in Turkey and kefta in Arabic countries. One dish, called shish kebabs, is made up of cubes of meat, tomatoes, and onions roasted on a metal rod.

Another Bite

In Arabic, the word *halal* means "permitted." Muslims eat halal meat and other foods.

"Shish kebab" is the only Armenian term used in the English language. ▽

Middle Eastern "Sandwiches"

Pita bread isn't just used as a side dish or with dips. It holds food. Falafel is a ball of mashed chickpeas that has been spiced and fried in oil. It's especially popular in Israel, Syria, Qatar, and Egypt. Falafel is stuffed into pita and served with yogurt or tahini, a sauce made from sesame seeds.

Shawarma is another Middle Eastern "sandwich." Meat, often lamb or goat, is slowly roasted over a fire. Thin slices are wrapped in pita, spread with hummus or tahini, and topped with vegetables.

Another Bite

In Turkey, shawarma is called doner kebab. Doner means "turning." Kebab means "meat."

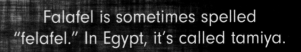

shawarma

Falafel is sometimes spelled
"felafel." In Egypt, it's called tamiya.

17

Salads

There are many kinds of Middle Eastern salads. They aren't like American salads. Tabbouleh, the national dish of Lebanon, is a salad made of tomato, mint, and **bulgur**. It's scooped up with lettuce leaves. Fattoush is a salad of bread and vegetables. It's also especially popular in Lebanon. Couscous is a tiny pasta that is used like rice. All kinds of ingredients may be added, such as carrots and raisins. Like other Middle Eastern dishes, the **recipe** changes with each cook!

fattoush

Though tabbouleh is thought to have been first made in Lebanon, it's popular all over the world now.

Time for Dessert

Just like in other parts of the world, desserts are sweet treats in the Middle East. Turkey is famous for its phyllo **pastry**. Layers of nuts and phyllo are used for desserts such as baklava. Qatayef are another special treat. Sometimes called "Arabic pancakes," they're filled with sweet cheese or nuts. Dates and halwa—a sticky mix of brown sugar, eggs, honey, and spices—are common desserts in Oman. In the Middle East, dessert is served with tea or a sweet, thick coffee.

baklava

Recipe:
Hummus
(requires the help of an adult)

Ingredients:
2 (16-ounce) cans of chickpeas

1/4 cup tahini (can be found in stores)

1/8 teaspoon salt

1 to 2 cloves garlic

juice of one lemon

Directions:
1. Drain and rinse chickpeas.
2. Put garlic, tahini, and salt in a blender. Blend until the ingredients are well mixed.
3. Add chickpeas (one can at a time) and blend after each addition.
4. Add lemon juice and blend.
5. Put in a bowl and sprinkle with any extra spice you'd like, such as paprika or cumin.
6. Eat with pita or vegetables.

Glossary

barley: a kind of grain

barter: to exchange goods or services in return for other goods or services

bulgur: dried wheat

civilization: people living in an organized way

culture: the beliefs and ways of life of a group of people

fragrant: having a pleasant smell

ingredient: a part of a mixture

irrigation: the watering of a dry area by man-made means in order to grow plants

pastry: a mix of flour, water, and fat used for desserts such as pies

recipe: an explanation of how to make a food

religion: a belief in and way of honoring a god or gods

For More Information

Books

Behnke, Alison. *Cooking the Middle Eastern Way: Culturally Authentic Foods Including Low-Fat and Vegetarian Recipes.* Minneapolis, MN: Lerner Publications, 2005.

Steele, Philip. *The Middle East.* Boston, MA: Kingfisher, 2006.

Websites

Middle Eastern Civilizations

www.kidspast.com/world-history/0042-middle-eastern-civilizations.php

Learn about the many civilizations that began in the Middle East.

Top 10 Middle Eastern Recipes for Beginners

mideastfood.about.com/od/middleeasternfood101/tp/beginnerrecipes.htm

Try making some of the most popular Middle Eastern dishes at home.

Index